D1377668

Published in 2014 by The Rosen Publishing Group, Inc.
29 East 21st Street, New York, NY 10010

Photo Credits: **KEY** tl=top left; tc=top center; tr=top right; cl=center left; c=center; cr=center right; bl=botto left; bc=bottom center; br=bottom right; bg=background

DT = Dreamstime; GI = Getty Images; iS = istockphoto.com; PDCD = PhotoDisc; SH = Shutterstock; TF = Topfoto; wiki = Wikipedia

front cover GI; **1**c TF; **4–5**cl TF; **6**bg iS; bl, c, cl, cr TF; **6–7**c TF; **7**bg iS; cr, tl, tr TF; **10**bl, br, tl iS; tl TF; bl wiki **11**bl, br, tl, tl, tr iS; bl, tr TF; **12–13**c iS; **13**tr iS; bc SH; cr, tc TF; **14**bc iS; bl, **14–15**c TF; **15**bc iS; bc, bl, cr, TF; **16**bl, tl TF; **17**cr, tl TF; **18**bc iS; bc, tl TF; **19**bc iS; tc TF; **20**bl TF; **20–21**c TF; **21**cl SH; br TF; **22**bc, cl TF; **23**br iS; **24**bc iS; bc, cr, tl TF; **25**br iS; cr SH; tl TF; **26**bl, tr iS; bl TF; **26–27**bc iS; **27**tr DT; c PDCD; br SH; **28**bl TF; **28–29**c TF; **29**br, tr TF; **30**bg iS; **31**bg iS; **32**bg TF

All illustrations copyright Weldon Owen Pty Ltd. **27**c Steve Karp

Weldon Owen Pty Ltd
Managing Director: Kay Scarlett
Creative Director: Sue Burk
Publisher: Helen Bateman
Senior Vice President, International Sales: Stuart Laurence
Vice President Sales North America: Ellen Towell
Administration Manager, International Sales: Kristine Ravn

Library of Congress Cataloging-in-Publication Data

Brasch, Nicolas.
 The Industrial Revolution : age of invention / by Nicolas Brasch.
   p. cm. — (Discovery education: discoveries and inventions)
 Includes index.
 ISBN 978-1-4777-1332-7 (library binding) — ISBN 978-1-4777-1506-2 (pbk.) — ISBN 978-1-4777-1507-9 (6-pack)
 1. Invention—Juvenile literature. I. Title.
 T48.B783 2014
 609—dc23
                          2012043617

Manufactured in the United States of America

CPSIA Compliance Information: Batch #S13PK3: For Further Information contact Rosen Publishing, New York, New York at 1-800-237-9932

THE INDUSTRIAL REVOLUTION
AGE OF INVENTION

NICOLAS BRASCH

PowerKiDS press

New York

Contents

An Era of Invention 6

Before the 1700s 8

Steam Engine 10

Electric Light................................ 12

Sewing Machine.................................. 14

Reaper 16

Mechanical Calculator......................... 18

Telegraph 20

Telephone.. 22

Pasteurization 24

Combustion Engine 26

Movie Camera 28

Glossary.. 30

Index 32

Websites 32

An Era of Invention

The 1800s was a period when people with ideas transformed human life. At the start of the century, there were no electric lights, no trains, no cars, and no way to communicate long distances without hand-delivering messages. By the end of the 1800s, scientific discoveries were curing diseases, houses and streets were lit by electric lights, people traveled long distances in trains, cars were beginning to replace horses on the streets, and when people wanted to send a message they picked up the telephone.

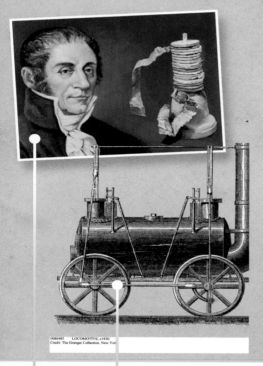

LOCOMOTIVE, c1830.
Credit: The Granger Collection, New York

1800
Alessandro Volta, an Italian physicist, was a leader in the study of electricity. In 1800, he invented a device called the voltaic pile that stored electricity until it was required for use. This was the first battery.

1814
George Stephenson was an English engineer who built his first locomotive in 1814. It was designed to carry coal away from a mine. He went on to build railroads and, with his son Robert, more efficient and powerful steam trains.

1829
William Burt was an American inventor and politician who invented a machine that had alphabetical characters on a rotating frame. He named it the typographer, and this led others to develop the typewriter.

1837
Samuel Morse, an American artist, was an unlikely inventor. Overhearing a conversation gave him the idea to see if messages could be sent using electromagnets. The result was the telegraph. Its first message sent was, "What hath God wrought."

1856
Louis Pasteur was a French chemist who made many major discoveries. One of these was pasteurization, which involves heating liquids, such as milk, to a point where harmful microorganisms are killed, but the liquid does not spoil.

1866
Alfred Nobel was a Swedish businessman who invented dynamite. This was important for the mining industry because it made blasting rocks safer and more efficient. Criticism of his invention led Nobel to establish the Nobel Prizes.

1876
Alexander Graham Bell was a Scottish scientist and engineer, and one of several people who claimed to have invented the telephone. Influenced by Morse's telegraph, he figured out how to send complex signals to reproduce voice.

1885
Karl Benz was a German engineer who made a major contribution to the development of the motor vehicle. He invented several engine-powered vehicles, including a motorized tricycle. In 1886, he built the first fuel-powered car.

Before the 1700s

Environmental impact
Before the 1700s, most farms were small and self-sufficient. Only enough food was grown or reared to feed a family or small community. As a result, little environmental damage was done to the land.

Threshing
This involved beating grains, such as corn, to separate edible seeds from nonedible parts of the plant.

Small–herd farming
Some farmers still breed just a few animals that they graze on rich land. This is the method used to produce high-quality cheese.

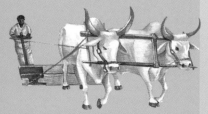

Plowing
Tractors have replaced oxen to pull plows in many countries, but not in some developing areas.

H umans have been farming and digging the ground for around ten thousand years. For most of that time, the work has been slow and backbreaking. It is only in the last 200 to 300 years that technology has enabled farmers and workers to carry out their tasks with enough speed and ease to transform their work and their lives.

Some cultures do not have the money, knowledge, or resources to invent, build, or buy the technology that would enable them to live an easier, less physical life. They still work the ground as their ancestors did for generations.

Field one
In fall, oats, barley, and other crops are ready for harvesting.

Understanding the land

In northern Europe, it is traditional to rest some of the land each year so it recovers the nutrients that it lost from growing crops. This helps to ensure that when new seeds are sowed, the land produces good-quality crops.

A HELPING HAND

In ancient China, farmers did not keep many large animals because it meant having to use valuable land to grow fodder for livestock. They did recognize, however, that some animals could make their work a lot easier, such as those that could pull heavy iron plows.

Oxen pulling a plow

Field two
This field has been left alone to recover its nutrients.

Field three
This field is being plowed and sowed for next summer's wheat harvest.

Vintage
Grapes are being crushed to make wine.

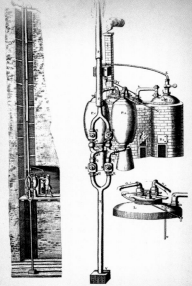

Steam Engine

The steam engine was one of the most important inventions in history. It converted energy into motion, and this motion was used to power machines. Before the steam engine, most of the power used in farming and other industries came from humans and animals.

The steam engine worked by burning coal to boil water. The boiling water produced steam that drove a moving piston. This piston was connected to other parts of a machine that performed useful work or drove a vehicle forward.

Thomas Savery, 1698
One of the first steam engines was invented and built by Englishman Thomas Savery in 1698. It did not have a piston but used a method of heating then cooling water to pump water out of coal mines.

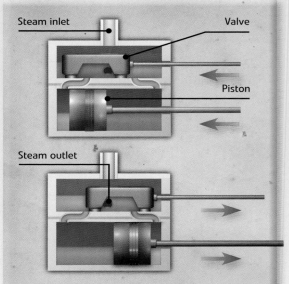

James Watts, 1769
The steam engine that did the most to bring on the Industrial Revolution was invented by James Watts. His double-acting steam engine piped pressurized steam (red) to a cylinder that drove the piston. The engine also had an outlet that allowed exhaust steam (blue) to escape.

Thomas Newcomen, 1712
Thomas Newcomen also invented a steam engine to pump water out of mines. His version did have a piston. This piston was attached to a rod. When the rod moved, it raised or lowered a chain that was attached to a pump.

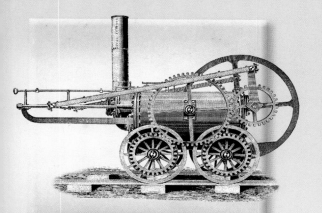

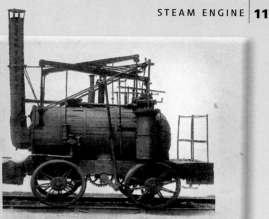

Richard Trevithick, *c.* 1800
Richard Trevithick was determined to build a high-pressure engine in which the boiler and engine were inside the same device. His success, in around 1800, enabled him to build a locomotive that paved the way for others to produce faster, more efficient steam trains.

Puffing Billy, 1813
The world's oldest surviving steam locomotive is *Puffing Billy*. It was built in 1813 to transport coal from a coal mine. It was so heavy that it could travel at a top speed of only 5 miles per hour (8 km/h). Yet it was more efficient than the horses that lugged coal up until that time.

Robert Stephenson, 1820s
With his father, George, Robert Stephenson set up the first company in the world to build steam-powered locomotives. They improved on the designs of other inventors and, by the mid-1820s, their engines easily won races that were held between various inventors.

Steam power, mid–1800s
By 1850, high-pressure steam engines were powering factories and mills in developed countries. The boiler was heated with coal or wood and quickly heated the water piped into it. A flywheel smoothed the delivery of power to the machines.

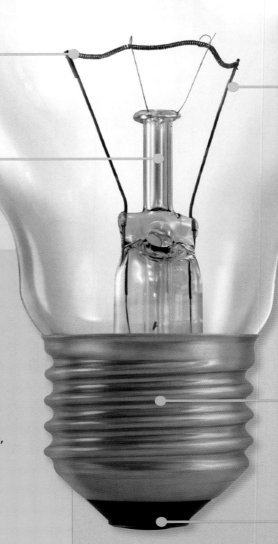

Driven by heat
Incandescent lightbulbs work by producing enough heat to create light. This is why they are very hot to touch. It also makes them inefficient because about 90 percent of the energy that is produced is lost through heat.

Filament
The coiled wire along the top is called the filament. It is made from tungsten, a metal with a very high melting point.

Glass mount
A glass mount with two wires on top help to support the filament.

Electric Light

The incandescent electric lightbulb was invented independently by various people in the 1800s. Thomas Edison's long-lasting and practical design was tested in 1879 and had a huge impact.

Apart from being far more convenient than gas lamps or candlelight, lightbulbs proved to be lifesavers in some industries. In mining, for example, deaths commonly occurred when dangerous gases came into contact with the naked flames held by miners to see where they were going and what they were doing.

Inert gas
The glass bulb is filled with an inert gas, which does not react when the filament heats up and helps to prolong filament life.

Wires
Two wires connect the filament to the metal contacts at the base of the bulb.

Screw base
This enables the bulb to be screwed into a fixture. There are also bayonet bases that fit into different types of fixtures.

Electrical contacts
Located at the base of the bulb are the electrical contacts that connect with the electricity supply.

Humphry Davy
A British scientist and inventor, Humphry Davy studied the properties of gases. In 1802, he demonstrated the first incandescent light by passing current through a platinum strip. He also invented a miner's lamp that enclosed the flame to prevent an explosion of dangerous methane gas in the mine.

Thomas Edison
An American scientist and inventor, Thomas Edison made the biggest breakthrough in the invention of the incandescent lightbulb. He used a carbon filament, which heated up and produced light. The first public demonstration of this took place on December 31, 1879.

ENERGY EFFICIENT
Fluorescent lightbulbs are much more efficient than incandescent lightbulbs because they produce light rather than heat. They work by having electrons collide with mercury atoms, which then produces ultraviolet, or UV, light. Since UV light cannot be seen by humans, phosphor powder on the tube turns this into visible light.

A fluorescent lightbulb

Sewing Machine

The invention of the sewing machine in the mid-1800s dramatically changed life, both in the home and at work. Large-scale textiles factories sprang up, with workers expected to produce garments many times faster than they had by hand. It provided work for many workers who did not have the skill to make clothes by hand.

With such production methods, clothes also became cheaper to buy for the people who previously made their own clothes because they could not afford to buy them.

Early machine
Isaac Singer founded the Singer Manufacturing Company, and this is one of its first sewing machines, made in 1851.

Isaac Singer
Although Isaac Singer did not invent the sewing machine, he certainly made it more accessible. One of his ideas was to pack the sewing machine inside a box so it could act as a stand when not in use.

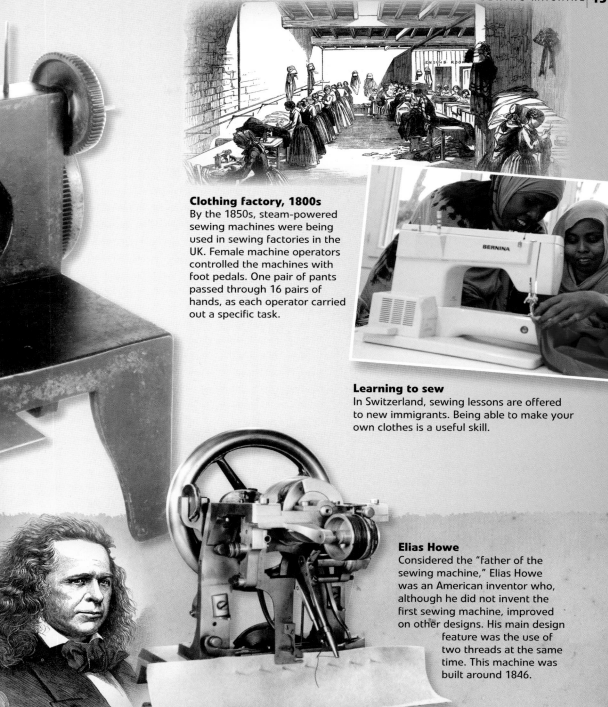

Clothing factory, 1800s
By the 1850s, steam-powered sewing machines were being used in sewing factories in the UK. Female machine operators controlled the machines with foot pedals. One pair of pants passed through 16 pairs of hands, as each operator carried out a specific task.

Learning to sew
In Switzerland, sewing lessons are offered to new immigrants. Being able to make your own clothes is a useful skill.

Elias Howe
Considered the "father of the sewing machine," Elias Howe was an American inventor who, although he did not invent the first sewing machine, improved on other designs. His main design feature was the use of two threads at the same time. This machine was built around 1846.

Reaper

Before the invention of the reaper in the 1830s, cutting crops was backbreaking work. For many farm workers, it involved bending down and using a sickle to cut the plants at their base. The lucky ones had the longer-handled scythes, so did not have to bend quite so far. However, it was still very hard work.

Apart from making the task of cutting crops easier, the reaper also collected the crops. This eliminated another stage in the production of crops that had previously been done by hand.

Cyrus McCormick
Cyrus McCormick was an American farmer and inventor whose mechanical reaper transformed farming practices. His father began the invention but handed it over to Cyrus, who demonstrated the first working mechanical reaper in 1831.

Divider
This separated the grain so it could be cut.

Reel mechanism
This held the grain in place while it was being cut, and pushed the cut grain onto the platform.

Mechanical reaper
Cyrus McCormick's mechanical reaper was invented on the family property, Walnut Grove Farm, in Virginia. The wide wheel in the center carried the weight of the machine and also operated the cutting blade.

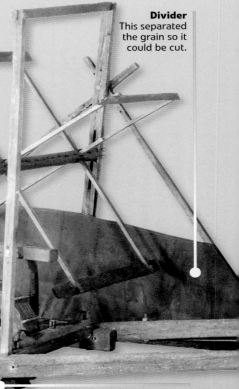

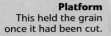

Platform
This held the grain once it had been cut.

Drive wheel
This was attached to the cutting blade. As the wheel turned, the blade cut.

Labor saver
The mechanical reaper meant that the job of reaping crops required only two people: one to manage the horses, and the other to rake up grain that fell off the platform.

Combine harvester
The combine harvester is the modern version of the mechanical reaper. It was invented in 1834 by Hiran Moore and combines three processes: cutting, threshing, and cleaning grain.

Cut grain is stored in the grain tank.

Grain is loaded onto trailers through the unloading tube.

Rotating blades cut the grain.

Wooden poles
These were hitched to the horse team that pulled the reaper.

Did You Know?
The invention of the mechanical reaper meant that two people could cut 12 acres (4.9 ha) of grain a day, compared to 4 acres (1.6 ha) a day with a scythe.

Mechanical Calculator

The computer is thought of as a twentieth century invention, but the idea for a machine that could process complicated calculations goes back much farther. In the 1820s, an English mathematician, Charles Babbage, decided to invent a machine that could calculate mathematical tables.

As a mathematician, Babbage was annoyed by the high error rate of other people in doing such calculations. He began designing mechanical calculators in 1822, although he never completed one. Nevertheless, his progress and the notes he made led to his designs being completed by other inventors more than 100 years later.

Charles Babbage
In 1824, Charles Babbage was awarded the Gold Medal by the Royal Astronomical Society in London for his invention of an engine that calculated mathematical and astronomical tables. The Society must have been impressed by his idea because he had only just started developing his machine at that time.

COW CATCHER

Charles Babbage did complete some inventions. Among them was a metal frame that was attached to the front of train engines to clear the track of obstacles. The invention's real name was the pilot, but it became popularly known as the cow catcher.

A model steam locomotive with a cow catcher

Analytical engine

In the 1830s, Charles Babbage started building a mechanical calculator he called an analytical engine. His design suggested it would be 15 feet (4.6 m) tall and 6 feet (1.8 m) wide. He never completed it, but part of it is held in the Science Museum in London.

Modern computer
The first functioning mechanical calculators were built in the 1930s. Once built, technology and ingenuity led to the invention of electronic machines, which led to the invention of the computer. Today, more than 1 billion computers are used around the world.

Telegraph

Today, messages are sent around the world in a flash. People can speak directly with each other, and even watch each other as they communicate. Until the 1830s, the only way to send a message from one place to another was by foot or on horseback. Then the telegraph was invented, and messages could be sent and received much quicker. The telegraph was based on the principles of electromagnetism and involved using electrical pulses to produce different signals, which could be decoded into letters and words.

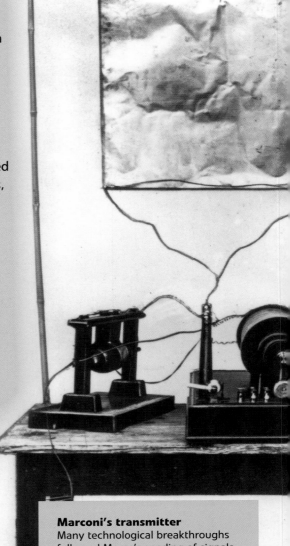

Samuel Morse
Samuel Morse's idea for the telegraph came to him while on a boat trip from the United States to the UK. He overheard some passengers talking about electromagnets and wondered whether they could be used to send messages through metal wires.

Marconi's transmitter
Many technological breakthroughs followed Morse's sending of signals using electric currents. Among them was the radio. This transmitter was used by the Italian inventor, Guglielmo Marconi, to send radio signals across the Atlantic Ocean.

HOW TO USE MORSE CODE

Samuel Morse invented a code where each letter of the alphabet was represented by a series of short or long electrical pulses. These pulses became commonly known as dots and dashes. People trained in Morse code would receive the pulses and then decode them into messages.

The Morse code alphabet

This chart shows which dots and/or dashes represent which letters of the alphabet. Apart from the letters, the period and comma are also represented, as is a query for when the receiver of the message does not understand one of the signals.

A .−	N −.	0 −−−−−
B −...	O −−−	1 .−−−−
C −.−.	P .−−.	2 ..−−−
D −..	Q −−.−	3 ...−−
E .	R .−.	4 ....−
F ..−.	S ...	5 .....
G −−.	T −	6 −....
H	U ..−	7 −−...
I ..	V ...−	8 −−−..
J .−−−	W .−−	9 −−−−.
K −.−	X −..−	Period .−.−.−
L .−..	Y −.−−	Comma −−..−−
M −−	Z −−..	Query ..−−..

In an emergency

SOS is a signal that someone sends when they need urgent help. The letter "S" is represented by three dots, while "O" is represented by three dashes.

Commercial use

In the telegraph operating room of the Western Union Company in New York messengers delivered the intended message to one of the operators, who then tapped the Morse code signals on the small machine on the table.

Telephone

Few inventions have changed human communication to the same extent as the telephone. This device works by converting sound, in the form of a human voice, into an electrical signal transmitted along a wire, then back into a form that sounds like the original voice.

Several people have been associated with the invention of the telephone, but the main two are Scotsman Alexander Graham Bell and American Elisha Gray. Amazingly, they both filed patent claims for the telephone on the same day, February 14, 1876.

Bell and Watson
The first message sent by telephone was from Alexander Bell to his assistant, Thomas Watson. They were in different rooms of the same house. The message is believed to have been, "Come here, Watson. I want you."

Candlestick phone
The first telephones were known as candlestick phones and had no numbers to dial. Instead, callers were connected to receivers by an operator.

Early telephone

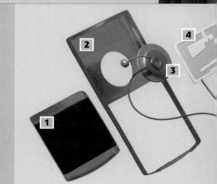

The exchange

The place where operators connected callers and receivers was called an exchange. Operators received calls from the caller and connected them manually to the receiver. The first exchange was opened in 1877 in Connecticut. Manual exchanges were still common in the mid-1900s.

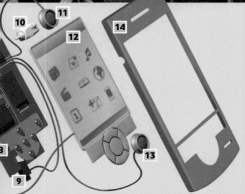

Cell phone

The cell phone was invented in the 1970s but recent technological improvements mean it is now a versatile communication device, not just a tool for sending and receiving voice messages.

1 Battery	**6** Circuit board	**10** Vibrator
2 Back case	**7** Microchip	**11** Speaker
3 Camera	**8** Button contacts	**12** Touch screen and display
4 Antenna	**9** Headphone socket	**13** Microphone
5 SIM card		**14** Front case

Pasteurization

Pasteurization is a process that involves heating a liquid so that harmful bacteria are killed, but the flavor of the liquid is not affected. It was discovered by a French chemist, Louis Pasteur, in 1864. Before this process was discovered, the only way to kill the bacteria was to boil the liquid, but this usually destroyed the flavor.

The most common liquid that is treated by pasteurization is milk. However, the process was originally developed to prevent microorganisms from causing wine and beer to go sour.

Louis Pasteur
Frenchman Louis Pasteur made many scientific breakthroughs. He created a vaccine for rabies and discovered that infectious diseases are caused by microorganisms. Known as the "father of microbiology," his work in this field led to others discovering the cure to many diseases.

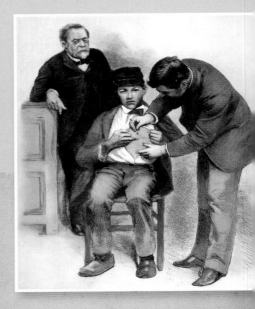

Pasteurization in the 1800s
By the late 1800s, the process of pasteurizing milk became widespread. As milk was passed through heating instruments, harmful microorganisms were destroyed and the shelf life of milk was extended.

Rabies vaccine
Rabies is a deadly viral disease that affects the nervous system. It is most commonly transmitted through the bite of a rabid animal, such as a pet dog. The invention of Louis Pasteur's vaccination helped to save many lives.

Batch method pasteurization
In small milk-packaging companies, the process of pasteurizing milk involves raw milk being poured into a huge pasteurization vat, where it is heated. It is then cooled and stored before being transported to stores. Meanwhile, the vat is washed and readied for the next batch.

Continuous method pasteurization
Large dairies and milk-packaging companies use a process known as continuous method pasteurization. This involves milk passing through a series of pipes and plates that are heated to the required temperature. This is much faster and more efficient than the batch method.

Did You Know?
Pasteur's work led to a concept known as the germ theory of disease. This concept explains how germs attack humans from outside the body.

Antiseptic aid
Pasteur's realization that diseases could be avoided by preventing microorganisms from entering the body led Joseph Lister to develop the idea of applying antiseptics before medical procedures.

Combustion Engine

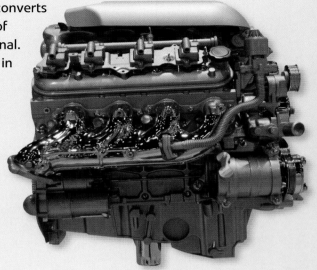

The combustion engine is a device that converts heat into motion. There are two types of combustion engines: external and internal. The first combustion engine was developed in the 1600s and was a tube with gunpowder in the bottom and a piston in the top. When the gunpowder was lit, it exploded, causing the piston to move. However, the piston could move only once before the tube had to be refilled with gunpowder.

The first combustion engines that worked well enough to be produced on a mass scale were invented in the 1860s by Jean Joseph Étienne Lenoir from Belgium and Nicklaus Otto from Germany.

EXTERNAL ENGINE

A steam engine is an example of an external combustion engine. The burning process takes place outside the engine—in this case, in a boiler. The steam passes through pipes until it reaches the pistons that drive the wheels.

The Northumbrian steam engine built by George and Robert Stephenson in 1830.

Internal engine
The most common type of internal combustion engine is the car engine. This four-stroke engine was invented by Nicklaus Otto. With internal combustion engines, the process of converting heat into motion takes place inside the engine.

How a four-stroke engine works

The four-stroke internal combustion engine has four different cycles that each perform a different function. These cycles are known as intake, compression, combustion, and exhaust. The aim of the process is to move the piston so it can drive motion outside the engine.

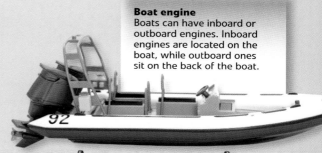

Boat engine
Boats can have inboard or outboard engines. Inboard engines are located on the boat, while outboard ones sit on the back of the boat.

Intake valve

Piston

Chamber

Spark plug

Crankshaft

Exhaust valve

1 Intake
The piston is at the top of the chamber. As the intake valve opens, the piston moves down, letting air and fuel be drawn into the chamber.

2 Compression
The piston moves upward, compressing air and fuel. At the same time, the valve closes, increasing the pressure in the chamber.

3 Combustion
When the piston reaches the top of the chamber, the spark plug ignites the fuel-air mixture. The explosion forces the piston down, and this causes the crankshaft to turn.

4 Exhaust
When the piston reaches the bottom of the chamber, the exhaust valve opens, and the piston pushes the fumes up and out. When the piston reaches the top, the process begins again.

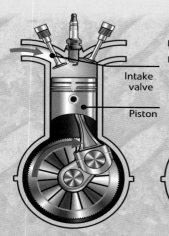

Lawn mower engine
These have two- or four-stroke internal combustion engines. Pulling the cord causes fuel and air to start entering the engine's chamber.

Motorbike engine
Most of these use a two-stroke engine, in which the intake and exhaust cycles are incorporated in the compression and combustion cycles.

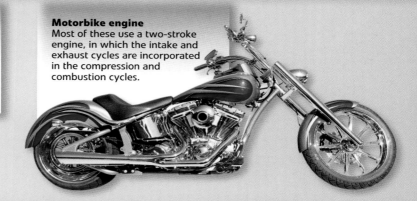

Movie Camera

Movie cameras work by projecting still images at a very fast speed, creating the illusion of movement. It is no surprise then that many of the earliest inventors of movie cameras had a background in still photography.

From the moment it was first revealed to the public, this ability to project moving images onto screens transformed popular culture. When you consider the popularity of movies and television today, it is hard to imagine what entertainment would have been like before the invention of the movie camera.

Lumière brothers
Among those credited with inventing the first movie camera are the Lumière brothers, Auguste and Louis, from France. Their interest in photography and film came from working in their father's photographic business. They invented their first movie camera in 1894.

First Lumière camera
What made the Lumière camera stand out from similar inventions around the same time was that it functioned as a camera, film processing unit, and projector in one. It was called the Cinématographe and advanced the processed images at 16 frames per second.

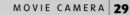

Public screenings
The Lumière brothers held public screenings of their films from 1895. The first film they made showed workers leaving the Lumière family's photographic factory at the end of the day.

KINETOSCOPE ARCADE

Thomas Edison, who invented the incandescent lightbulb, also invented the kinetoscope, a cabinet with a peephole. When people looked though the peephole, they saw pictures moving rapidly.

Inside a kinetoscope arcade in California in 1894.

Glossary

analytical
(a-nuh-LIHT-ih-kul) Able to investigate and work out something complicated.

bacteria
(bak-TIR-ee-uh) Single-cell microscopic life forms, only a few of which are harmful.

edible (EH-deh-bul)
Describes something that can be eaten.

electromagnetism
(ih-lek-troh-MAG-nuh-tih-zum) Branch of physical theory concerned with electricity and magnetism.

eliminated
(ih-LIH-muh-nayt-ed)
Removed or expelled.

fluorescent
(flu-REH-sent) Giving off one color of light using the energy of light of a different color or wavelength.

flywheel (FLY-weel)
A heavy wheel that resists change in speed to ensure the smooth operation of machines.

fodder (FAH-der)
Low-quality food for animals.

incandescent
(in-kan-DEH-sent) Giving off a temperature that causes it to produce light.

inert (ih-NERT)
Describes something that does not react chemically.

ingenuity
(in-jeh-NOO-ih-tee)
Cleverness.

mill (MIL) A building where raw materials are combined to create a different, finished product.

nutrient (NOO-tree-ent)
Something that provides energy when it is eaten.

piston (PIS-tun) A cylinder or disk that fits into a larger, hollow cylinder and moves under pressure.

plow (PLOW)
A tool used to dig up the ground.

pressurized
(PREH-shuh-ryzd) Under a great deal of pressure.

rabies (RAY-beez)
An infectious disease passed on by animals.

self–sufficient
(self-suh-FIH-shunt) Able to support oneself without outside help.

sickle (SIH-kul)
A handheld agricultural tool with a curved blade that is used to cut crops.

vat (VAT)
A large container, often used for storing or processing liquids.

Index

B
Babbage, Charles 18, 19
battery 6, 23
Bell, Alexander Graham 7, 22
Benz, Karl 7
Burt, William 6

C
cell phone 22, 23
Cinématographe 28
combine harvester 17
combustion engine 26, 27

D
Davy, Humphry 13

E
Edison, Thomas 12, 13, 29

G
Gray, Elisha 22

H
Howe, Elias 15

I
Industrial Revolution 10

L
Lenoir, Jean Joseph Étienne 26
lightbulb 12, 13, 29
Lister, Joseph 25
Lumière, Auguste 28, 29
Lumière, Louis 28, 29

M
Marconi, Guglielmo 20
McCormick, Cyrus 16
mechanical calculator 18, 19
Moore, Hiran 17
Morse code 21
Morse, Samuel 6, 7, 20, 21
movie camera 28, 29

N
Newcomen, Thomas 10
Nobel, Alfred 7

O
Otto, Nicklaus 26

P
Pasteur, Louis 7, 24, 25
pasteurization 7, 24, 25
plowing 8, 9
Puffing Billy 11

R
rabies 24
reaper 16, 17
Royal Astronomical Society 18

S
Savery, Thomas 10
sewing machine 14, 15
Singer, Isaac 14
sowing 9
steam engine 6, 10, 11, 26
Stephenson, George 6, 11
Stephenson, Robert 6, 11

T
telegraph 20, 21
telephone 22, 23
Trevithick, Richard 11
typographer 6

V
Volta, Alessandro 6
voltaic pile 6

W
Watts, James 10

Websites

Due to the changing nature of Internet links, PowerKids Press has developed an online list of websites related to the subject of this book. This site is updated regularly. Please use this link to access the list: www.powerkidslinks.com/disc/revo/